W9-AVN-699

© 2002 Algrove Publishing Limited
ALL RIGHTS RESERVED.
No part of this book may be reproduced in any form, including photocopying, without permission in writing from the publishers, except by a reviewer who may quote brief passages in a magazine or newspaper or on radio or television.

Algrove Publishing Limited
1090 Morrison Drive
Ottawa, Ontario
Canada K2H 1C2

National Library of Canada Cataloguing in Publication Data

Streeter, Robert A
    Are you a genius? / by Robert A. Streeter and Robert G. Hoehn ; with illustrations by O. Soglow.

(Classic reprint series)
Reprint of ed. originally published: New York : F.A. Stokes Co., 1932.
ISBN 1-894572-59-9

1. Puzzles. 2. Psychological recreations. I. Hoehn, Robert G II. Title.
III. Series: Classic reprint series (Ottawa, Ont.)

GV1493.S77 2002   793.73   C2002-903625-9

Printed in Canada
#10902

Publisher's Note

The common criticism of I.Q. tests is that they are unfair if used cross-culturally because they inevitably are biased in favor of the creator's culture. The tests in this reprint have not only a cultural bias but a temporal bias. They are biased in favor of American readers who were born before WWI. Even so, many 21st century readers will find they score well compared to the rich and famous used as standards by the authors. Regardless of result, be assured that there is no valid measurement of I.Q. taking place as readers try the enclosed tests.

Leonard G. Lee, Publisher
Ottawa
August, 2002

ARE YOU A GENIUS?

ARE YOU A GENIUS?

??

By
ROBERT A. STREETER
AND ROBERT G. HOEHN

With Ten Illustrations by
O. SOGLOW

FREDERICK A. STOKES COMPANY
NEW YORK   MCMXXXII

COPYRIGHT, 1932, BY FREDERICK A. STOKES COMPANY

All rights reserved. No part of this work may be reproduced without the written permission of the publishers.

PREFACE

VICE PRESIDENT MARSHALL said, "What this country needs is a good five-cent cigar." We really disagree with Mr. Marshall and feel that perhaps a few more Geniuses might prove to be the salvation. So we have set about to create some.

Incidentally this little book provides entertainment of a sort that has been popular throughout the ages in that it matches wits. Most of the questions are psychological in type—they require a mind that resembles an active mountain goat rather than a saturated sponge. In other words they necessitate agility of mind rather than book learning.

A few of the questions will be recognized as old favorites which probably caused nervous disorders several generations ago. To the unknown, deceased geniuses who originated them we extend thanks and sing praises after having feebly attempted to emulate their ability in creating mental confusion and psychic chaos among men.

We must also acknowledge with profuse appreciation the assistance and patience of the faculty and students of the Kingsley School, who have martyred themselves by acting as our experimental victims. They have lived, much like the superstitious man who walks in a cemetery at midnight, in fearsome apprehensive terror of being suddenly jumped out upon by an ogre—in the form of one of the authors with an evil smile and a catch question. We wish, too, to extend our thanks to those who have so generously permitted us to publish their scores, which stand as mute testimonials to their status as Geniuses. Their few errors can be interpreted only as verification of the statement of Francis Bacon: "A sudden, bold, and unexpected question doth many times surprise a man and lay him open."

THE AUTHORS.

CONTENTS

ANSWERS (*continued*)

INTRODUCTION

My introduction to mind-twisters was in 1887. I had, as you know, captured Geronimo (the first catch of that sort with a twelve-pound cotton line) singlehanded. One night, as my prisoner and I sat before our fire of Saratoga chips on the banks of the Rio Grande, the old Red put to me the problem of the man who wished to cross a river with a fox, a goose, and a peck of corn but whose rowboat would hold only one of these commodities and himself. After a few hours of argument in pure Apache, Geronimo made it clear to me that if the fox were left alone with the goose, one would eat the other, and if the goose were left with the corn, the same thing, so to speak, would happen.

What was not so clear to me was the solution, although Geronimo had it worked out to his own satisfaction. He would have the man cross with the goose and leave it (tethered, of course), next bring over the corn and carry back the goose, then ferry over the fox to be left with the corn and, finally, give the goose its third and last voyage. Always a lover of the concrete, Geronimo's diagrams were Einstein to me. I demanded a demonstration. We had the river and easily made a rowboat. A goose was purchased at the nearest poultry show. Corn came from the rich orchards which line the Rio Grande. A fox was something else, but I soon ran a fine specimen of the genus Vulpes to earth and the experiment began. All went well until Crossing No. 3—the fox and I. Suspecting that he was being taken for a ride, the creature leaped upon me and the boat capsized. When I got back to land, Geronimo was gone and General Miles had arranged a court-martial for me. (See War Dept. Reports, No. x5432-9876.) In later years I tried to interest brain-twirlers in the problem, but new ingredients are required. The modern man has a Jane, a gigolo and ten grand to transport.

I have been asked to indicate the easiest puzzle in this lovely book. It is the one about the man who has a four gallon and a seven gallon measure and must dish out exactly five gallons. To anybody who has tried, with the aid only of a gallon jug and a quart bottle, to mix perfectly two quarts of ethyl alcohol and three quarts of water and have the jug and the bottle filled with Gordon water all ready for the party such problems are elementary.

H. I. PHILLIPS, *Sun-Dial.*

ARE YOU A GENIUS?

HOW TO FIND A GENIUS

Sneak up on your friends and spring the questions on the following pages. For all except the last question in each group, score the one who answers first correctly one point. The final question in each group is a "brain-twister" and is worth three points. High score discloses the Genius.

If you have no friends, try the test by yourself, recording your time. In this case each of the first nine questions counts ten. The last one counts thirty. If you equal or better the score and time made by the notable whose name and grade appear before the test, you may be very certain that you are a Genius. If you find that you are not a Genius, don't be discouraged—remember "It's only a step from Genius to Insanity."

VITAL SERVICES THAT "ARE YOU A GENIUS" PERFORMS FOR YOU

1. Assures you that the beautiful girl whom you intend to marry is capable of supporting you.

2. Provides grounds for committing your mother-in-law to the insane asylum.

3. Locates any size 6 hat.

4. Determines your I. Q., if any.

5. Informs you what even your best friend won't tell you, that you have "mens debilis" (weak mind).

6. Provides a logical reason for committing suicide.

TEST I.

TEST NO. 1

Possible Score....... 120
Mr. Thomas' Score.. 100
Mr. Thomas' Time..   5 minutes, 20 seconds

Lowell Thomas is probably best known to the general public through his stories of true adventure, and as a radio commentator on the day by day adventures of mankind. His "With Lawrence in Arabia," "The Sea Devil," etc., were best sellers and are still widely read. Mr. Thomas is also distinguished as a lecturer and editor. He accompanied the Prince of Wales on a tour of India in 1922. He also did several years exploring in India, Upper Burmah, Malaya and Central Asia. In 1926 he made a 25,000 mile flight, the longest passenger airplane journey up to that date.

FOR EXPLANATION OF SCORING SEE PAGE 13

TEST 1

1. Rearrange the following letters so as to make the name of a living creature:
   BRINO

2. Four men can build four boats in four days. How long will it take one man to build one boat?

3. Test your memory on this passage.

   Three men and their wives and a widower left by automobile at noon one day for a picnic. After they had gone three miles, they saw two men and a child in a car that had broken down. "That is tough luck," said one of the picnickers. At one o'clock they arrived at the picnic grounds, where they saw only the old one-armed caretaker and his son. They immediately started to eat their luncheon of sandwiches, fruit and cake.

   Ques.: How many people have been mentioned?

4. The hands of a clock indicate that the time is 1:20. If the hour hand were where the minute hand is and vice versa, what time (to the nearest five minutes) would it be?

5. Which is heavier, milk or cream?

6. A man starts from a given point. If each time that he takes two steps forward he must take one backward, how many steps will he have to take in order

17

to reach a point five steps ahead of his starting point?

7. What one word means both "dodge" and "immerse"?

8. Excluding pennies, how many different combinations of coins will make 30¢?

9. What is the fallacy in the following interesting story told by an aviator?

   During the war I watched a friend of mine who was flying alone on an observation flight above the lines. When he had completed his mission and was on his way home, thinking to himself how lucky he was not to have seen an enemy plane, an Austrian aviator suddenly swooped upon him from above a cloud bank, and shot him to the ground. He was dead when the first person reached him.

"Brain Twister"

10. A fruit vender had a basket of oranges. A customer approached him and purchased one-half of the oranges plus one-half of an orange. A second customer came and bought one-half of what he had left plus one-half an orange. A third customer purchased one-half of what was then left plus half an orange. After this sale the vender had no oranges. He had not cut or broken an orange. How many did he have when he started?

TEST NO. 2

Possible Score...... 120
F. P. A.'s Score..... 100
F. P. A.'s Time.... 3 minutes, 10 seconds

Franklin P. Adams (F.P.A.) edits "The Conning Tower" for the New York Herald Tribune and is one of America's most distinguished writers and critics. His column is known internationally.

TEST 2

1. Mr. Addison Simms of Seattle was asked by his wife to purchase for her some supplies. She wrote a list which included condensed milk, coffee, salt, crackers, butter, eggs, and ham. Unfortunately Mr. Simms lost the list and returned home with eggs, ham, butter, coffee, salt, and condensed milk. What had he forgotten?

2. A can dig a ditch in three days. B can dig the same ditch in 6 days. How long will it take them working together to dig it?

3. What fraction (within 1/10) of a piece of floating ice is under water?

4. If 6 and 3 are 9, answer "wrong" unless 6 and 3 are not 8, in which case answer "right."

5. If the eleventh day of the month falls on Tuesday, what day of the week will the 30th be?

6. What is the largest number that can be made by re-arranging the digits in the number
38,017?

7. What is the fallacy in the following story?
Mr. Drake was driving his car along a straight highway which led to his destination, a town in Florida, about twenty miles north of his starting

point. When he had gone approximately nineteen miles, a fast-moving car passed his. As a result his car was forced a couple of yards off the highway, thereby scraping its side against some protruding bushes. He stopped his car, and, as he was looking out of the window to ascertain whether any noticeable damage had been done by the bushes, he judged from the position of the sun that it was late in the afternoon and that he would have to hurry. A couple of minutes later he arrived at his destination, happy in the thought that he had escaped a possible serious accident.

8. What state in the Union beginning with M has nine letters?

9. A boy buys a bat and a ball for $1.10. If the bat costs him a dollar more than the ball, how much does he pay for the ball?

"Brain Twister"

10. Rearrange the letters in the word "Sleuth" to make another word.

TEST 3

TEST NO. 3

Possible Score 120
Princess Kropotkin's Score.... 80
Princess Kropotkin's Time.... 10 minutes

Princess Alexandra Kropotkin, a descendant of the first Czar of Russia, was born in that country and lived there during the recolution. At present she resides in New York and is married to an American. She lectures and writes on Russian politics and is a linguist and a fashion authority.

24

1. What word meaning "ship" would mean "small collections of water" if the letters were read backwards?
2. How many different three digit numbers can be made from the digits 1, 2, and 3?
3. In the year 1938, the first day of February falls on Monday. What day of the week does the last day of February fall on?
4. Which is the greatest distance?

    10 ft.   3½ yds.   124 inches

5. An inaccurate historian wrote the following account:

    The early American colonists were a liberty-loving people. Because of the conditions imposed upon them they held numerous public meetings to determine what course of action to pursue. At one of these gatherings Thomas Jefferson sounded the keynote of their attitude when, in a memorable speech, he said "Give me liberty or give me death." Benjamin Franklin, who officially represented the colonies in England and France, was another loyal colonist. While in England in 1775, just previous to the revolution, he wisely advised Englishmen against the policy then being employed by Charles II and his ministry. Satisfaction was not given to the colonists, however, and finally by the signing of the Declaration of Independence in New York, on July 4, 1776, these men signified definitely their determination to enjoy liberty.

    Ques.: What three errors in historical facts has the historian made?

6. It takes normally thirty minutes to fill a tank. If, however, a hole allows one-third of the water being poured in to escape, how long will it take to fill the tank?

7. B is to E as 2 is to what number?

8. If the word POD were printed in small letters, how would it read if viewed up-side down?

9. The police records of New York City state the following facts in relation to the gruesome murder of Mr. Adolphus Crane. Remember as much of the account as possible:

   The sergeant at the desk of the ninth precinct received the alarm in the form of a telephone message from Mr. Crane's butler, Whitney, at 2:10 in the morning. Whitney pleaded for speedy assistance, saying that he knew definitely who the murderer was. Detectives McCarthy and Blair were immediately dispatched to the house. They arrived at 3 o'clock. At 3:05 the sergeant received another call, which proved to be the detectives. They had discovered that Whitney had been murdered also. Killed by a shot through the head, he lay in a pool of his own blood. Mr. Crane's death had been caused by a severe beating on the head with a blunt object. The mystery was never unraveled. No clues were discovered. The murderer had effectually destroyed the only avenue of approach by killing poor Whitney.

   Ques.: Between what specific times must Whitney have been murdered?

"Brain Twister"

10. A man having a seven gallon measure and a four gallon measure and no other container of any description goes to a well to get exactly five gallons of water. How does he do it?

TEST NO. 4

Possible Score........120
Mr. O'Brien's Score.. 90
Mr. O'Brien's Time.. 8 minutes, 10 seconds

Frank M. O'Brien has had a long newspaper career. He has served on the Buffalo Express, The New York Press, The New York Herald, and The New York Sun. Since 1926 he has been editor of The Sun. In 1921 Mr. O'Brien was awarded, for his article, "The Unknown Soldier," the Pulitzer Prize for the best editorial. He is the author of "The Story of the Sun" and numerous short stories.

TEST 4

1. A man lived in a house that could be entered by only one door and five windows. Making certain that there was no one in the house one day, he went out for the afternoon. Upon his return, although the windows were still locked and unbroken and the door had not been forced, he discovered a thief in his house robbing it. If the thief did not use a skeleton key, or pick any of the locks, how did he get into the house?

2. If a clock is stopped for a minute every ten minutes, how long will it take the minute hand to complete a revolution?

3. Within an inch what is the distance around the base of an ordinary pint milk bottle?

4. A father is three times as old as his son. In ten years he will be twice as old. How old is the father at present?

5. What two 4 letter words pronounced the same but spelled differently mean "valley" and "curtain"?

6. If 1 = a, 2 = b, 3 = c, etc., what word of five letters does the following number make?

38,945

7. If viewed up-side down, what number would the following digits make?

61961

8. A is five inches taller than B.
   C is five inches shorter than A.
   What is C's height in relation to B's?

9. Listen carefully to the following extracts from the diary of Robinson Crusoe:

   August 17. Spent the day chiefly in gathering my plentiful harvest of barley. Found that my pit had entrapped for me a female goat and her kid.

   August 18. Due to rain I worked most of this day on perfecting my grindstone and arranging my tools.

   August 19. Because of continued wet weather, I worked on the tasks of the previous day and found that my new grindstone was quite serviceable.

   August 20. The weather was very hot. I devised a sort of umbrella to give me shade. I made it from the skin of the she-goat, which I had killed, the idea coming to me because of the discomfort caused by the sun beating on me all day.

   August 21. On this day after a shower in the morning I explored the island taking as my equipment my parasol, a hatchet, and a saw.

   Ques.: On how many days did it rain?

"Brain Twister"

10. Two volumes of a thousand pages each are arranged properly in a book case. Each volume is two inches thick including the covers, each of which is one-eighth of an inch thick. If a bookworm eats his way from page 1, volume 1, to page 1000, volume 2, what distance does he travel?

TEST NO. 5

Possible Score...... 120
Mr. Phillips' Score.. 90
Mr. Phillips' Time.. 9 minutes, 40 seconds

Harry Irving Phillips was in his early career the Managing Editor of the New Haven Register. Later he associated himself with the New York Globe as a columnist. Now Mr. Phillips conducts the "Sun Dial," popular column in The New York Sun. He is the author of "The Globe Trotter" and "The Foolish Question Book."

TEST 5

1. Does one two-inch pipe fill a tank of water at the same speed, less quickly, or more quickly than two one-inch pipes?

2. What adjective which means "pertaining to citizenship" spells the same from right to left as it does from left to right?

3. Mr. Smith, while out walking one day, recognized a boyhood friend whom he had not seen nor heard about for more than ten years. His friend, after greeting Mr. Smith warmly, said, "I suppose that you do not know that I am married to some one whom I met shortly after I lost track of you. Here comes my daughter now."

   "How do you do?" said Mr. Smith, addressing the little girl. "What is your name?"

   "I am named after my mother," replied the child.

   "Oh, so your name is Catherine, too," said Mr. Smith.

   "Yes," answered the girl, "but how did you know?"

   How did Mr. Smith know that the girl's name was Catherine?

4. If it is 11 A.M. Eastern Daylight Saving Time, what time will it be a half hour later by Central Standard Time?

5. Name a president of the United States whose last name begins with "F."

6. What number expressed in Roman Numerals will the letters V I X make when looked at in a mirror?

7. See how good a detective you are. Follow the facts of this murder mystery closely:

    A man who was living by himself in a house in an isolated rural district was discovered dead one morning by his friend who had been visiting him until ten o'clock on the previous evening. An investigation showed that he had died of a bullet wound and that another bullet, which had apparently missed him, had shattered the clock, the hands of which indicated two o'clock. It was definitely proved by the dead man's friend that the clock had been shot sometime after his departure from the murdered man's home. A known enemy of the dead man against whom there was strong evidence of guilt was acquitted when two reliable witnesses swore that he had been with them from midnight until noon of the next day at a spot ten miles from the murdered man's home.

    Ques.: What was the fallacy in acquitting the dead man's enemy?

8. I am the son of your father's sister. What relative am I of yours?

9. What one word means both
    1. a form of physical competition
    2. a large class of people distinguished by common characteristics.

"BRAIN TWISTER"

10. If a hen and a half lays an egg and a half in a day and a half, how many eggs will six hens lay in seven days?

TEST 6

TEST NO. 6

Possible Score........ 120
Mr. Chappell's Score.. 90
Mr. Chappell's Time.. 8 minutes, 50 seconds

George S. Chappell, one of America's leading humorists, is famous both under his own name and that of "Dr. Walter Traprock," whose "Cruise of the Kawa" attracted wide attention. Mr. Chappell is also the author of "Through the Alimentary Canal with Gun and Camera," and other successful books.

TEST 6

1. In a book of 100 leaves, what leaf is page 49 on?

2. The first syllable of the name of a well-known university is suggested by a word meaning "a kind of grain." The second syllable is suggested by a letter in the alphabet.
   What is the name of the university?

3. When seen in a mirror, which of the following words printed in capital letters will look the same as when viewed directly?

   MAN   TOOT   DEED

4. How many black squares are there on a checker board?

5. A man while coming out of the door of his house in the morning notices that the sun is just rising above the horizon on his left. On this day it will take the sun ten hours before it sinks below the opposite horizon. Upon returning while he is unlocking the door, the sun is still on his left and a quarter of the way above the horizon. Approximately how long has he been gone?

6. There are three doors to a house and three men who wish to enter them. They all enter at the same time, and no two men enter the same door together. How many possible ways are there for them to enter the house?

7. What word meaning "a short distance" means if read backwards (from right to left) "beloved creatures."

8. In a football game the ball is on the 12-yard line. The center passes it back 9 yards toward midfield to a kicker, who steps forward 2 yards to kick a drop-kick. When he kicks the ball, how far is he from the goal posts at which he is kicking?

9. Imagine three horizontal lines an inch apart, one directly under another. Then imagine three vertical lines also an inch apart, each cutting all three of the horizontal lines.
   How many squares do these lines form?

"BRAIN TWISTER"

10. A man has $1.15 in modern U. S. currency. However, he cannot make change for any coin up to and including a dollar (i.e., a nickel, a dime, a quarter, a half-dollar or a dollar). He has neither a dollar bill nor a silver dollar. What coins has he?

TEST NO. 7

Possible Score...... 120
Dr. Holt's Score.... 80
Dr. Holt's Time.... 7 minutes, 20 seconds

Hamilton Holt, LL.D., Litt. D., L.H.D., is an editor, author and educator. Between 1913 and 1921 he was the owner and editor of "The Independent." Since 1925 Dr. Holt has been the President of Rollins College and has been much before the public eye for the educational theories and reforms which he has introduced into that institution. In addition Dr. Holt has been much interested in movements for world peace and was president of the third American Peace Congress. He is a lecturer at the University of California and at Yale.

TEST 7

1. A man and wife had four married daughters, and each of these had four children. No one in the three generations had died. How many people were there in the family?

2. There were a group of boys on bicycles playing follow-the-leader. There were 4 boys in front of a boy, 4 boys behind a boy, and a boy in the middle. How many boys were there altogether?

3. If you were attempting to climb an icy hill, and if after every time you had taken two steps forward, you slid back one step, how many steps forward would you have to take to reach a point five steps in advance of the starting point?

4. How will the following sentence, attributed to Napoleon, read if you start with the last word and read all the letters and words backwards?
   "Able was I ere I saw Elba."

5. How many times is the numeral "1" used on a dollar bill to indicate its denomination?

6. Listen carefully.
   If Cantor is not the President of the United States, answer "Hoover"; unless Al Smith is not a Democrat, in which case answer "Republican."

7. See if you can detect any mistakes in the following extract from a traveler's diary:

   While traveling in South America recently, I was especially interested in the peoples of Chile, Peru, Brazil, and Colombia. I was delighted also to hear some of the stories about famous old explorers, such as DeSoto, who discovered the Mississippi, and Balboa, who discovered the Pacific, thereby carrying the Spanish flag to remote parts of this continent. The whole of South America is fascinating to me, but the five countries mentioned above appeal to me particularly.

8. Assume that the earth is a perfect sphere and that a band is stretched about the equator so that it fits snugly. If one foot were added to the length of the band, this additional length would cause the band to stand off a certain distance from the surface of the earth at all points. Would this distance be:

   imperceptible, a fraction of an inch, about 2 inches, or about 1 foot?

9. In the following word eliminate the second letter and every alternate letter thereafter. What word do the remaining letters form:

   Gleams

"Brain Twister"

10. The first part of the name of a certain make of automobile is suggested by a word meaning "call"; the second, by a word meaning "insinuation." What is the make of the car?

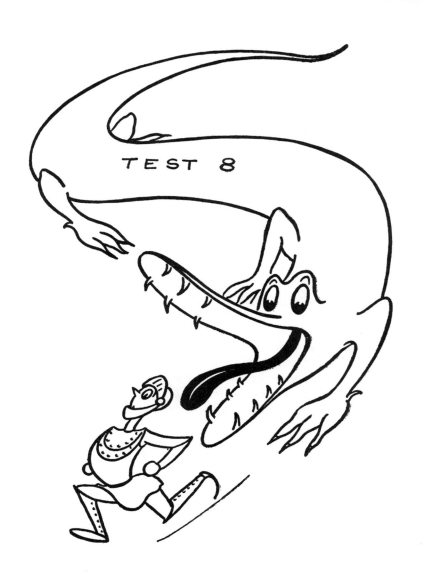

TEST 8

TEST NO. 8

Possible Score 120
Mr. Terhune's Score 110
Mr. Terhune's Time . . . .   9 minutes

Albert Payson Terhune is the author of many books, motion picture plays, stories and verses. As a young man he explored Syria and Egypt, investigating leper settlements, living among the desert Bedouins, etc. He is distinguished as a journalist, having been on the staff of the New York Evening World for over twenty years. At his beautiful country home "Sunnybank" in New Jersey he breeds prize-winning collies. His stories are known to all dog-lovers, including that perennial favorite "Lad: A Dog."

TEST 8

1. How do you pronounce "cho pho use"?

2. Listen carefully to the following story:

    At 5 A.M. on September 22, during the war, Private Jones had just been relieved as sentinel by his comrade. He became engaged in a conversation with his commander, Captain Smith. Just before he left after receiving some instructions, he remarked, "Well, sir, last night I dreamed that we weren't going to win this war, and my dreams seem always to come true."

    "Nonsense," replied the captain, "we've got to win and we've got to believe that we shall win. For once you're wrong."

    The captain, who was in a hurry to leave on his furlough, then dismissed the private. When he returned from his leave several days later, however, he had Private Jones courtmartialed.

    Why was Private Jones courtmartialed?

3. What one word means both "a means of conveyance" and "a procession"?

4. Which of the following liquid measures represents the smallest volume?

    2 gallons   9 quarts   17 pints

5. A watch indicates that the time is quarter of twelve. If the entire dial were moved around to the right a distance equivalent to five minutes, what time would the hands indicate?

6. The first two syllables of the name of one of the states of the United States is suggested by a girl's name. The third syllable is suggested by a word meaning "debark." What is the name of the state?

7. A starts from a given point and walks steadily at the rate of 3 miles per hour. B starts from the same point two hours afterward and walks in the same direction at the rate of 6 miles per hour. In what elapsed time, after A starts, does B overtake him.

8. There were 3 prisoners arraigned before a judge. The judge looked fiercely at the first and said, "What have you to say for yourself?"

The second one answered, "Not guilty, your honor."

The judge retorted sharply, "I wasn't speaking to you."

Whereupon the third one replied, "I didn't say anything."

How do you explain this strange procedure?

9. Rearrange the following letters so that they make the name of an article of furniture:

chocu

"BRAIN TWISTER"

10. You owe me 40 cents. In settlement I agree to buy from you for 60 cents a knife which is actually worth more. I give you 20 cents change and consider that we are even. However, I later discover that the knife that you gave me was stolen property, and in order to retain it, as I do, I must pay its original owner the full value of it, namely, 75 cents.

If I am not reimbursed by you for my loss, how much do I actually lose?

STRESSES AND DISTRESSES

HOW DO YOU PRONOUNCE?

I
Par—50%

1. comparable
2. penalize
3. gratis
4. inquiry
5. scion
6. cello
7. joust
8. gondola
9. heinous
10. oleomargarine

II
Par—60%

1. acclimate
2. sinecure
3. data
4. eczema
5. schism
6. chasm
7. quay
8. grimace
9. façade
10. flaccid

HOW DO YOU PRONOUNCE?

III
Par—60%

1. aviator
2. mischievous
3. impious
4. culinary
5. Pall Mall
6. orgy
7. bouquet
8. antipodes
9. vaudeville
10. sacrilegious

IV
Par—50%

1. epitome
2. precedence
3. incognito
4. jugular
5. zoölogy
6. gaol
7. hoof
8. apparatus
9. adult
10. antipode

SPELLING BEES

The following words are correctly spelled. Try them out on your friends.

I

Par—80%

1. all right
2. fiery
3. benefited
4. fulfilled
5. zephyr
6. sergeant
7. athlete
8. isthmus
9. attendant
10. superintendent

II

Par—50%

1. embarrass
2. naphtha
3. paraffin
4. liquefy
5. preceding
6. seize
7. siege
8. heinous
9. Philippines
10. Filipino

III

Par—50%

1. harass
2. picnicking
3. vilify
4. supersede
5. diphtheria
6. parallel
7. soliloquy
8. weird
9. hemorrhage
10. sacrilegious

LET THE GENIUS TRY THIS GROUP

IV

Par—30%

1. kaleidoscope
2. liaison
3. reconnoiter (re)
4. camouflage
5. xylophone
6. sassafras
7. connoisseur
8. rhododendron
9. hieroglyphics
10. bourgeoisie

THESE ARE EASY BUT TRY THEIR PLURALS

V

Par—70%

1. solo
2. banjo
3. crisis
4. stimulus
5. grouse
6. thief
7. beef
8. reef
9. soliloquy
10. cupful

Answers on page 100

JUGGLERS

JUGGLERS

1. Juggle the letters in each of these words to make another word:

    1. ring

    2. terse

    3. bored

    4. came

    5. scopes

2. Juggle each of these into two others:

    1. Hades

    2. slow

    3. salt

    4. rime

    5. slide

3. Juggle each of these into three others:

    1. span

    2. parses

    3. lead

    4. emit

    5. serve

4. Now juggle each of these into four others:

        1. pears

        2. steam

        3. stale

        4. stime

        5. risen

BLUNDERS

WHICH WOULD YOU SAY?

I

Par—60%

1. (Don't) (doesn't) he know you?

2. Everybody took (his) (their) seat(s).

3. Give it to (whoever) (whomever) wants it.

4. Measles often (has) (have) serious effects.

5. There (is) (are) a door and three windows.

6. Father asked Fred and (I) (me) to do the job.

7. He said that we seemed to be (them) (they).

8. (It's) (its) a fine day.

9. What do you think of (his) (him) winning the race?

10. She is one of those girls who (are) (is) usually sad.

WHICH WOULD YOU SAY?

II

Par—70%

1. This is a (healthy) (healthful) climate.

2. He is (likely) (apt) to come soon.

3. He is (likely) (liable) to help us.

4. He was (hanged) (hung) for treason.

5. He came (quite) (rather) early.

6. Yesterday I (lay) (laid) on the sofa for three hours.

7. The weather (effected) (affected) his health.

8. Slander has ruined his (character) (reputation).

9. The (discovery) (invention) of electricity was important.

10. He has (less) (fewer) studies now than he had.

WHAT'S YOUR I. Q.?

If you really want to get the dope on yourself, take these tests. Do it privately so that if your score is low, your wife won't know that her suspicions are verified. If, perchance, you score higher than Mr. Lenz or Mr. Dodd, whose scores are given on the following pages, we suggest that you tell your boss and touch him for a raise. He will undoubtedly be happily surprised to see signs of intelligence.

SCORE 5 POINTS FOR EACH QUESTION CORRECTLY ANSWERED

WRITTEN TEST NO. 1

Possible Score...... 100
Mr. Lenz's Score... 90
Mr. Lenz's Time... 18 minutes, 20 seconds

Sidney S. Lenz needs no introduction to bridge players anywhere. He is one of the greatest living experts of the game and the author of many books on the subject, of which "The One, Two, Three, Official System of Contract Bidding" is the latest. Mr. Lenz lives in New York City and is active on the editorial staff of "Judge."

WRITTEN TEST NO. 1

1. Not a few persons do not think it unnecessary not to be dishonest in their dealing with others.

   Does this mean the same as saying that many persons think it necessary to be honest in their dealings with others?

   (Write "yes" or "no" on your answer sheet.)

2. The hands of a clock which is set by Eastern Daylight Saving Time are in a position so as to form a straight line. If the minute hand is on the figure 1, what time will it be by Eastern Standard Time in ¾ of an hour?

3. "The man is a fox."

   Which one of the adjectives listed below could best be substituted for "a fox" so as to convey the same meaning:

   wise   hairy   greedy   quick   cunning

4. What one word means both:

   (a) mark of identification

   (b) torch

5. My father is the brother of your sister. What relative am I of yours?

   cousin   nephew   son   uncle   son-in-law

6. Read the following statement:

"The army stood like a stone wall." Which one of the words listed below best shows the quality common to both "army" and "stone wall"?

impenetrability   courage   hardness   permanency

7. If 117 is divisible by 3, write the number 3 on your answer sheet, unless 186 is divisible by 4, in which case write the number 5 on your answer sheet.

8. C is to 3 as F is to what number?

9. Read the following sentence:

"The pilot steered the ship of state over the rough sea of public sentiment."

Which of the statements below corresponds most nearly in meaning?

The captain managed his ship well in a terrible storm.

The pilot guided the President's yacht over a rough sea.

The President ran the government well in spite of adverse criticism.

66

10. In the following series how many numbers above 10 and below 20 are even?

6 25 10 5 19 11 22 9 12 18 20 33 16 21
13 14 15

11. What state of the Union that begins with "W" contains 9 letters?

12. Jack is three years younger than James. John is two years older than Jack. What is James' age in relation to John's?

   1 yr. younger   4 yrs. younger   1 yr. older
                        4 yrs. older

13. A person is a good friend if:
   1. He is true to you in time of need
   2. He lends you money
   3. He tells you that you are a good fellow

14. If 1 = a, 2 = b, 3 = c, etc., what word does the following number make:

25,138

15. By eliminating one letter in each of four words in the following sentence, a new sentence of an entirely different meaning will remain.

   They heard meat was stewed.

   Write on your answer sheet the new sentence.

16. If three men can build four boats in two days, at the same rate, how long will it take one man alone to build two boats?

17. By rearranging the letters in the word "plea" make three new words.

18. What one word in the following passage destroys the trend of thought?

   In preparing for an important fight, a boxer trains strictly. He must live regularly, eat carefully, and exercise strenuously. For weeks before an important battle he undergoes numerous privations and forgoes many pleasures. Nevertheless, if he is unsuccessful in his subsequent bout, he is disappointed because his training efforts have not brought him victory.

19. How many odd numbered circles are there below that do not contain any of the letters that appear in the word "anxious"?

20. In the circles below select the number from the largest circle containing an odd number and no letter which appears in the word "beat" and add it

to the number in the smallest circle which contains
one of the letters in the word "acabus." What is
the result?

WRITTEN TEST NO. 2

Possible Score 100
Mr. Dodd's Score . . 85
Mr. Dodd's Time . . 20 minutes, 40 seconds

Frank C. Dodd is President of the important publishing house of Dodd, Mead & Company, New York. Mr. Dodd has been active in the book business since his graduation from Yale in 1897. He served as President of The National Association of Book Publishers, and is regarded as one of America's leading publishers.

WRITTEN TEST NO. 2

1. A man shouts in the direction of a cliff which causes an echo that he hears 2 seconds later. If sound travels at the rate of 1100 feet per second, how far away is the cliff?

2. Which two of the following words are composed of the same letters:

agate	agitate	gates
stags	stage	grate

3. In the sentence below each dash represents an omitted letter. Write completely the words that contain dashes.

   M–r––es and s–a–ps often breed ––s–uit––s.

4. Jones earns more money than Smith. Doe's salary is less than Johnson's. Johnson earns more than Smith but less than Jones.

   Who gets the greatest salary?

5. If you had half as much money again in addition to what you have, you would have $1.20. How much have you?

6. What modern U. S. coin is the same size as the circle below?

7. Letting 1 = a, 2 = b, 3 = c, etc., write the number which denotes the word "hedge."

8. What word meaning "light blows" means, when it is read backwards, "gaiter"?

9. The sum of the digits of certain dates (years) in the 20th century up to the present time equals 13. What dates are these?

10. Write the following on your answer sheet and, by inserting two periods and a question mark, make the meaning clear.

    That that is is that that is not is not is not that so

11. What three numbers in the following series are divisible by 2, 3, 4, 6 and 8?

    64   66   48   52   74   24   88   32   96   16

12. Rearrange the following words into a true statement. Persons all geniuses insane are.

13. The first syllable of the name of an important city of the United States is suggested by a word meaning "harbor." The second syllable is suggested by a word meaning "earth." What is the name of the city?

14. In the following sentence one word obviously destroys the meaning. Write on your answer sheet the word which, if substituted for the one improperly used, would make the sentence logical.

    Since he was an honest man almost all his life, he was once guilty of stealing.

15. There are two different numbers between 1 and 10 the sum of which added to their product equals 35. What are the numbers?

16. In the following sentence, if the second word means "ascended," write the first word in the sentence on your answer sheet, unless the sixth word does not mean "quickly," in which case write the fourth word in the sentence on your answer sheet.

He climbed the steep hill rapidly.

17. What one word means both:
    a. a vehicle
    b. a platform?

18. How many different letters of the alphabet are used in the following sentence?

The quick brown fox jumps over the lazy dog.

19. Mark on your answer sheet the second highest number that you find on the figure below:

592	932	391	915
646	869	341	914
846	211	921	586
833	528	933	593

20. On the figure above locate number 914. Count three squares to the left and one square above. Take the last digit of the number in this square. Remember it. Now locate number 528. Count one square to the right and three squares above. Take the middle digit of this number. Remember

73

it. Now locate number 593. Count two squares to the left and one square above. Take the first digit of this number. Multiply this digit by the sum of the other two which you have in your mind. Write the result on the answer sheet.

MORONS' MORGUE

THE HORSE RACE

Maurice G. Michaels correctly solved "The Horse Race" in 4 minutes and 28 seconds.

Mr. Michaels has for many years been manager and book buyer of Brentano's, Inc., New York. Prior to that he served as instructor of English Literature in the city High Schools. He has also been a playwright, producer and theatrical manager. His first venture in the book business was as buyer for A. R. Womrath, Inc.

THE HORSE RACE

There were three horses running in a race. Their names were Tally-ho, Sonny Boy, and Juanita. Their owners were Mr. Lewis, Mr. Bailey, and Mr. Smith, although not necessarily in that sequence.

Tally-ho unfortunately broke his ankle at the start of the race.

Mr. Smith owned a brown and white three-year old.

Sonny Boy had previous winnings of $35,000.

Mr. Bailey lost heavily although his horse almost won.

The horse that won was black.

This race was the first race that the horse owned by Mr. Lewis had run.

What was the name of the horse that won?

THE MARINERS

Richard Van Rees correctly solved "The Mariners" in 9 minutes and 16 seconds.

"Cap'n" Dick, as he is familiarly known by Long Island yachtsmen, is president of the Van Rees Corporation, one of the largest book manufacturers in America. Mr. Van Rees is the skipper of the yacht "Vanitie," winner of several cup races in Great South Bay.

THE MARINERS

There are three ships, the "Albatross," the "Americus," and the "Hispaniola," on the sea sailing for the ports of Liverpool, New York, and Cherbourg, but not necessarily in that order. They are commanded by Captains Brine, Tarr, and Salt.

A few months ago Captain Tarr was the guest of Captain Brine on the "Albatross."

The "Hispaniola" hit a derelict on her last crossing and as a result, for seven weeks previous to the present trip, was in dry dock for repairs.

The "Albatross" has just passed the "Americus" in mid-ocean and shipped a stowaway back by the "Americus."

Mrs. Salt, who usually travels with her husband, was yesterday discharged from the hospital where she was treated for a week for a severe attack of ulcers of the stomach. This unfortunate condition victimized her while she was three days from land and necessitated her immediate removal to the hospital when the ship docked.

The Captain of the "Americus" is preparing a report for his owners, Cartright and Smith, Ltd., of Liverpool, which he will have to deliver to their offices as soon as the ship docks.

What ship does Captain Tarr command and to what port is it bound?

THE MURDERED CARD PLAYER

Ellery Queen correctly solved "the Murdered Card Player" in 3 minutes and 30 seconds.

"Ellery Queen" is the pen name of the great mystery detective writer whose books have been among the best selling mystery stories of recent years. While his identity must remain a secret, his stories are known to all mystery fans. His book, "The Greek Coffin Mystery," has attracted wide attention.

THE MURDERED CARD PLAYER

Four men, whom we shall call Robert, Ronald, Ralph and Rudolph, were playing cards one evening. As a result of a quarrel during the course of the game, one of these men shot and killed another. From the facts given below, see if you can determine who the murderer and his victim were.

Robert will not expose his brother's guilt.

Rudolph had been released from jail on the day of the murder, after having served a three-day sentence.

Robert had wheeled Ralph, a cripple, to the card game at Ronald's house.

Rudolph had known Ronald for only five days before the murder.

Ralph had met Robert's father only once.

The host is about to give evidence against the murderer, whom he dislikes.

The murdered man had eaten dinner on the previous night with one of the men who did not bowl with Ronald customarily.

SCORES ON "THE FOOTBALL TOURNAMENT"

Two scores are given for this last and probably the hardest problem in ARE YOU A GENIUS?

Lawson Robertson correctly solved "The Football Tournament" in 14 minutes and 32 seconds.

Mr. Robertson occupies a very prominent position in the sporting world. Since 1914 he has been track coach at the University of Pennsylvania. In the 1924, 1928, and 1932 Olympic Games Mr. Robertson has been the head coach of the U. S. Track and Field event contestants. In addition he has been trainer to the University of Pennsylvania football teams.

Ellis W. Meyers correctly solved "The Football Tournament" in 12 minutes and 49 seconds.

Mr. Meyers has been for many years the efficient Executive Secretary of the American Booksellers Association and is well known to booksellers and publishers throughout the United States.

THE FOOTBALL TOURNAMENT

An elimination tournament in football was held in which four colleges—Trinity, Tufts, Temple, and Tulane —participated. The winners of the first two games met in the third and final game to decide the championship. The colors of the various teams were brown, blue, red, and purple, and the competing captains were Albie, Barry, Bill, and Ben, though not necessarily respectively. From the facts given below, answer the following questions:

Who defeated whom in the play-off, and by what score?

Who was the captain of each team?

What was the color of each team?

---

1. In the final game Albie's team made its only score by a touchdown on the first play, but missed the point after touchdown.
2. The red team lost to Tufts in the first game.
3. Ben's team defeated Tulane 12 to 0.
4. The captain of the purple team saved his team from being scoreless in the third game by a 40-yard field goal.
5. Ben's team did not play Trinity.
6. Barry's team lost to the undefeated team.
7. Albie did not see his former friend, the captain of the brown team.

ANSWERS

ANSWERS—TEST 1

1. Robin

2. 4 days

3. 12

4. 5 minutes after 4 o'clock

5. Milk, because cream comes to the surface.

6. 11 steps

7. Duck

8. 5 combinations—6 nickels
   3 dimes
   quarter and a nickel
   4 nickels and a dime
   2 nickels and 2 dimes

9. No one could possibly know of what the aviator was thinking because his death occurred before he could have told any one of his thoughts.

10. 7 oranges.

ANSWERS—TEST 2

1. Crackers

2. 2 days

3. 9/10

4. Right

5. Sunday

6. 87,310

7. The fallacy is that Mr. Drake, who must have been looking out of the window on the right side of his car to see any possible damage, could not have seen the sun on that side while he was traveling north.

8. Minnesota

9. Five cents

10. Hustle

ANSWERS—TEST 3

1. Sloop

2. 6 combinations: 123   213   312
                   132   231   321

3. Sunday

4. 3½ yds.

5. 1. Patrick Henry, not Thomas Jefferson, said, "Give me liberty or give me death."
   2. In 1775 George III, not Charles II, was King of England.
   3. The Declaration of Independence was signed in Philadelphia, not New York.

6. 45 minutes

7. 5—B is the second letter in the alphabet and E is the fifth.

8. The same. Pod.

9. Between 2:10 and 3 o'clock.

10. He fills up the 4-gal. measure and pours it into the 7-gal. measure. Then he refills the 4-gal. container and pours from it into the 7-gal. container as much as the latter will hold, or 3 gallons. This operation leaves him with 1 gal. in the 4-gal. measure. He completely empties the 7-gal. container and pours the 1 gal. into it. Then he again fills the 4-gal.

88

measure and empties it into the 7-gal. measure which gives him the desired 5 gals.

or

He fills up the 7-gal. measure and from that he fills the 4-gal. measure, leaving 3 gals. in the 7-gal. measure. Then he empties the 4-gal. measure and pours the 3 gals. from the 7-gal. container into the 4-gal. container. Next he fills again the 7-gal. measure and from it fills the 4-gal. container. He now has 6 gals. in the 7-gal. measure. Then he empties the 4-gal. measure and refills it from the 6 gals. in the 7-gal. container, leaving him 2 gals. in the 7-gal. measure. Again he empties the 4-gal. container and transfers the 2 gals. that are in the 7-gal. container to the 4-gal. measure. Filling up the 7-gal. container again, he transfers from it the 2 gals. necessary to fill the 4-gal. measure. This operation leaves him with the desired 5 gals. in the 7-gal. measure.

ANSWERS—TEST 4

1. He entered the door which the man had left unlocked.

2. 65 minutes.

3. 9¾ inches (exact measurement).

4. The father is 30 years old.

5. Vale, veil.

6. Chide.

7. 19,619.

8. It is the same.

9. 3 days.

10. ¼ inch. When standing on a bookshelf in proper order, volume 2 is at the right of volume 1, making page 1 of volume 1 separated from page 1000 of volume 2 only by the two covers.

ANSWERS—TEST 5

1. A 2-inch pipe fills the tank more quickly than two 1-inch pipes. The area of the mouth of the 2-inch pipe is twice as great as the sum of the areas of the mouths of the two 1-inch pipes, as may be ascertained by applying the formula—area of a circle.

2. Civic.

3. Mr. Smith's boyhood friend was a woman named Catherine and the mother of the girl.

4. 9:30 A.M.

5. Millard Fillmore, the 13th President, inaugurated in 1850.

6. XIV   14.

7. The basis of the acquittal was that the clock that had been shot fixed the time of the murder at 2 A.M., at which time the acquitted man proved definitely that he was ten miles from the scene of the murder. However, if the clock had stopped at 2:00 on a previous day and was not running when it was shot, it would not indicate the time of the murder. Nor would it have fixed the time of the murder if the murderer had set it at 2 o'clock after shooting it. The deed could have been committed by the acquitted man between the hours of 10 and 12 o'clock when no investigation of his whereabouts was made.

8. Cousin.

9. Race.

10. 28 eggs. The common mistake that is made is figuring that 1 hen lays 1 egg in 1 day and that the answer, therefore, is 42. Actually, each hen lays only 1 egg in a day and one-half or 2/3 of an egg in a day.

ANSWERS—TEST 6

1. The 25th leaf.

2. Cornell.

3. TOOT.

4. 32 black squares.

5. Approximately 7½ hours.

6. In 6 different ways.
   Explanation: The squares below represent the doors. The men are numbered 1, 2, and 3 respectively. They might enter the doors in any of the following combinations:

	□	□	□
1.	1	2	3
2.	1	3	2
3.	2	1	3
4.	2	3	1
5.	3	1	2
6.	3	2	1

7. Step.

8. 29 yards (the goal posts are 10 yards behind the goal line).

9. 4 squares.

10. He has a fifty-cent piece, a quarter, and four dimes.

1. 26 people.

2. 5 boys.

3. 8 steps.

4. "Able was I ere I saw Elba."

5. 10 times.

6. "Hoover."

7. There is only one mistake in the extract. He has named four countries and later referred to them as five.

8. The band would be almost 2 inches (1.91 inches) away from the earth at all points.

This at first seems inconceivable and is not clear until one realizes that the radius of any circle, *regardless of its size,* must increase 1.91 inches if 12 inches are added to the circumference. This may be proved geometrically by the application of the following formula: circumference equals twice the radius $\times$ 3.1416. For purposes of simplification, using "C" for "circumference," "R" for "radius" and "3" for "3.1416," we arrive at the following:

$$C = 2 \times R \times 3 \text{ or } R = \frac{C}{2 \times 3} \text{ or } R = \frac{C}{6.}$$

Let us apply this formula to a small circle measuring 6 inches in circumference: $R = \frac{6,}{6,}$ or the radius

= 1 inch. Now let us increase the circumference by 12 inches or make it 18 inches.

$R = \dfrac{18}{6,}$ or radius = 3 inches, which is a 2 inch increase. In the same manner let us find the radius of a circle 12 feet or 144 inches in circumference:

$R = \dfrac{144}{6,}$ or radius = 24 inches. Now let us increase the circumference by 12 inches to 156 inches.

$R = \dfrac{156}{6,}$ or radius = 26 inches, an increase of 2 inches. It is therefore apparent that the radius of any circle will increase approximately 2 inches when 12 inches are added to the circumference. The same is theoretically true of a band representing the circumference of the earth. A 12 inch increase in circumference would cause a 2 inch increase in radius. The 2 inch increase in radius would make the band stand out from the surface of the earth 2 inches at all points.

9. Gem.

10. Chrysler (Cry slur).

ANSWERS—TEST 8

1. Chop-house.
2. The sentinel had been sleeping during his duty.
3. Train.
4. 2 gallons.
5. Twenty minutes before eleven o'clock.
6. Maryland.
7. 4 hours.
8. The judge was cross-eyed.
9. Couch.
10. Sixty cents.

STRESSES AND DISTRESSES—ANSWERS

I

Word	Usual Mispronunciation	Proper Pronunciation
1. comparable	com par'a ble—accent on second syllable	com' par a ble—accent on first syllable
2. penalize	short "e" as in "pen"	long "e" as in "feet"
3. gratis	short "a" as in "rat"	long "a" as in "grate"
4. inquiry	ĭn' quĭ ry—accent on first syllable	ĭn quī' ry—2nd "i" long as in "fine"—accent on 2nd syllable
5. scion	skeon	"c" not pronounced — sion—"i" as in "fine"
6. cello	"c" as "s"	"c" as "ch" in "chin"
7. joust	"ou" as in "out"	pronounced "joost" or "just"
8. gondola	gŏn dō' la—accent on 2nd syllable	gŏn' dŏ la—accent on 1st syllable
9. heinous	"ei" pronounced as "i" in "fīne"	"ei" pronounced as "a" in "hay"
10. oleomargarine	soft "g" as in "gym"	hard "g" as in Margaret

II

Word	Usual Mispronunciation	Proper Pronunciation
1. acclimate	ăc′ clĭ māte—accent on 1st syllable	ăc clī′ māte—accent on 2nd syllable—"i" as in "fine"
2. sinecure	"i" short as in "sin"	"i" long as in "fine"
3. data	first "a" short as in "rat"	first "a" long as in "date"
4. eczema	ĕk zē′ ma—accent on 2nd syllable and long 2nd "e"	ĕk′ zĕ ma—accent on 1st syllable and short "e" in 2nd syllable
5. schism	"sch" pronounced as "sk" or "sh"	"sch" pronounced as "s" —sism
6. chasm	"ch" as in "chew"	kăsm
7. quay	kwāy	kēy
8. grimace	grĭm′ ĭs	gri māce′ "a" as in "face"—accent on last syllable
9. façade	"c" as "k"—2nd "a" long as in "made"	"c" as "s"—2nd "a" is broad as in "Ah"
10. flaccid	"cc" as "ss"—flăssĭd	first "c" as "k"—2nd "c" as "s"—flak′ sĭd

97

III

Word	Usual Mispronunciation	Proper Pronunciation
1. aviator	1st "a" short as in "have"	1st "a" long as in "gave"
2. mischievous	mĭs chēēv′ ius—extra syllable and accent on 2nd syllable	mĭs′ chĕv ous—accent on 1st syllable
3. impious	ĭm pī′ ous, accent on 2nd syllable, 2nd "i" long as in "pine"	ĭm′ pĭ ous, accent on 1st syllable, 2nd "i" short as in "pig"
4. culinary	"u" short as in "cull"	"u" long as in "cupid"
5. Pall Mall	paul maul	pĕll as in "pelt"; mĕll as in "melt"
6. orgy	hard "g" as in "get"	soft "g" as in "gym"
7. bouquet	"ou" as "o" bō-kāy	"ou" as "oo"—bōō-kāy
8. antipodes	silent "e"; accent on 1st syllable—an′ tĭ podes	pronounce "e" long as in "me"—accent on 2nd syllable — ăn tĭp′ o dēēs
9. vaudeville	"au" as "awe"; 1st "e" pronounced — vau dah vil	"au" as "o" in "vōcal"; 1st "e" not pronounced—vōd′ vĭl
10. sacrilegious	săc′ rē lĭ gius	săc′ rĭ lē gius, "e" long as in "be"

98

IV

Word	Usual Mispronunciation	Proper Pronunciation
1. epitome	accent on 1st syllable —ĕ' pĭ tōme and silent "e" in last syllable	accent on 2nd syllable; last "e" pronounced long as "me"—ĕ pit' ō mē
2. precedence	accent on 1st syllable; 2nd "e" short as in "end"—prĕ' cĕ dĕns	accent on 2nd syllable; 2nd "e" long as in "eke"—prē cē' dĕns
3. incognito	accent on 3rd syllable; 2nd "i" as "ee"—ĭn cŏg nēē' tō	accent on 2nd syllable; 2nd "i" short as in "nip"—ĭn cŏg' nĭ tō
4. jugular	first "u" as in "jug"	first "u" as "oo"
5. zoology	first "o" as "oo"	first "o" long as in "go" —zō ol' o gy
6. gaol	gōle or gāle	jail
7. hoof	"oo" as in "hook"	"oo" as in "choose"
8. apparatus	3rd "a" short as in "rat"	3rd "a" long as in "rate"
9. adult	accent on first syllable—a' dult	accent on 2nd syllable— ă dult'
10. antipode	"e" long as in "mē"; accent on 2nd syllable—an tip' ō dēē	silent "e"; accent on 1st syllable— ăn' tĭ pode

SPELLING (PLURALS)—ANSWERS

1. solos
2. banjos
3. crises
4. stimuli
5. grouse
6. thieves
7. beeves
8. reefs
9. soliloquies
10. cupfuls

JUGGLERS—ANSWERS

1

1. ring—grin
2. terse—steer
3. bored—robed
4. came—mace
5. scopes—copses

2

1. Hades—heads, shade
2. slow—lows, owls
3. salt—slat, last
4. rime—emir, mire
5. slide—sidle, idles

3

1. span—pans, snap, naps
2. parses—spares, spears, sparse
3. lead—dale, deal, lade
4. emit—mite, time, item
5. serve—verse, veers, sever

4

1. pears—parse, spear, pares, rapes, spare
2. steam—meats, mates, teams, tames
3. stale—least, tales, slate, teals, steal
4. stime—times, mites, items, smite
5. risen—resin, siren, rinse, reins

BLUNDERS—ANSWERS

I		II	
1.	doesn't	1.	healthful
2.	his seat	2.	likely
3.	whoever	3.	likely
4.	has	4.	hanged
5.	are	5.	rather
6.	me	6.	lay
7.	they	7.	affected
8.	it's	8.	reputation
9.	his	9.	discovery
10.	are	10.	fewer

WHAT'S YOUR I. Q.?—ANSWERS
Written Test No. 1

1. Yes.
2. 6:50; 10 minutes before 7 o'clock.
3. Cunning.
4. Brand.
5. Nephew.
6. Impenetrability.
7. 3.
8. 6.
9. The president ran the government well in spite of adverse criticism.
10. Four.
11. Wisconsin.
12. One year older.
13. He is true to you in time of need.
14. Beach.
15. The hard mat was sewed.
16. Three days.
17. Leap, peal, pale.
18. Nevertheless.
19. 2.
20. 7.

WHAT'S YOUR I. Q.?—ANSWERS

Written Test No. 2

1. 1100 feet.
2. Gates, stage.
3. Marshes, swamps, mosquitoes.
4. Jones.
5. 80 cents.
6. Penny.
7. 85475.
8. Taps.
9. 1903, 1912, 1921, 1930.
10. That that is is. That that is not is not. Is not that so?
11. 48, 24, 96.
12. All insane geniuses are persons.
    (Or) Insane geniuses are all persons.
    (Or) Insane geniuses all are persons.
13. Portland.
14. Though or although.
15. 3 and 8.
16. He.
17. Stage.
18. 26.
19. 932.
20. 22.

MORONS' MORGUE—ANSWERS

The Horse Race

Mr. Smith's horse could not have won, because the horse that won was black.

Mr. Bailey's horse did not win.

Therefore, Mr. Lewis's horse must have won.

Tally-ho could not have won, and so could not have been Mr. Lewis's horse, because he broke his ankle at the start; and Sonny Boy could not have been Mr. Lewis's horse because he had previously run.

Therefore, Juanita must have been Mr. Lewis's horse, the winner.

The Mariners

Brine is Captain of the "Albatross" because he was host to Tarr on that ship.

It is obvious from the statement about Mrs. Salt that her husband's ship has not been in dry dock just previous to this trip because she was taken off of it, ill, eight days ago when it landed.

Therefore, Salt's ship cannot be the "Hispaniola," which has been in dry dock for seven weeks, and must be the "Americus."

Tarr's ship then is the "Hispaniola."

The last statement of the problem shows that the "Americus" is headed for Liverpool.

The "Albatross" must have New York for its destination because the fact that it shipped a stowaway back by the "Americus" proves that it was going in the opposite direction to the "Americus."

Therefore, the "Hispaniola" must be bound for Cherbourg.

MORONS' MORGUE ANSWERS

The Murdered Card Player

The first statement makes it plain that Robert's brother is the murderer, and Robert then is innocent.

Ralph cannot be Robert's brother because he has met Robert's father only once. Therefore Ralph is not guilty.

Ronald, the host, since he is about to give evidence against the murderer, cannot be the murderer.

Therefore, Rudolph must be the murderer.

Since the host, Ronald, is about to give evidence, he must still be alive; and Rudolph, the murderer, obviously cannot be the victim.

This leaves as the murdered man either Robert or Ralph.

Since Ralph is a cripple and since Rudolph has known Ronald for only five days, they are the men with whom Ronald did not customarily bowl; so one of them must have eaten with the murdered man on the night previous to the murder. Rudolph was in jail and so it was not he. Then Ralph must have eaten with the victim.

Ralph then is not the victim, and since Rudolph and Ronald have both been previously eliminated, Robert is obviously the murdered man.

Then Rudolph murdered Robert.

MORONS' MORGUE ANSWERS

The Football Tournament

From statement (1), Albie's team made its only score in the final game by a touchdown; from statement (4), the purple team scored only a field goal in this game. Therefore Albie's team beat the purple team 6-3 in the play-off.

Statement 3 shows that Ben's team survived the first round by defeating Tulane and must, therefore, have been the purple team, which was defeated by Albie's team in the play-off.

Knowing the above facts and from statements (3) and (6), we can now bracket the teams thus:

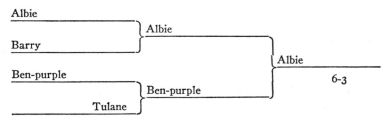

It is now obvious from the brackets that Bill must have been captain of Tulane.

From the brackets also we see that Tulane was the only team that Albie's team did not meet. Statement (7) proves that Tulane was the brown team.

THE FOOTBALL TOURNAMENT—*Continued*

Our brackets are now filled out as follows:

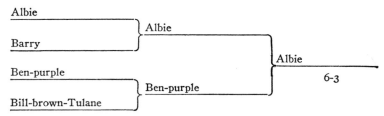

From statement (2), it is apparent that the red team must have been Barry's and that Albie's team was Tufts.

Since we have found that the red, purple, and brown teams were Barry's, Ben's, and Bill's respectively, Albie's team must have been blue.

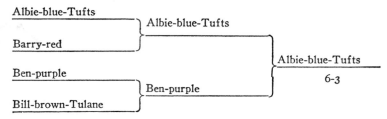

As Trinity did not play Ben's team (statement (5)), the brackets show us that Trinity was Barry's team.

Therefore, Ben's team must have been Temple.

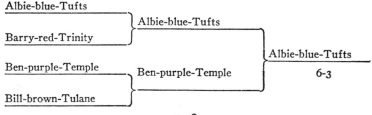